SPOTLIGHT ON NATIVE AMERICANS

AZTEC

Erin Long

PowerKiDS
press.

New York

Published in 2016 by The Rosen Publishing Group, Inc.
29 East 21st Street, New York, NY 10010

First Edition

Editor: Sarah Machajewski
Book Design: Samantha DeMartin
Reviewed by: Robert J. Conley, Former Sequoyah Distinguished Professor at Western Carolina University and Director of Native American Studies at Morningside College and Montana State University. Supplemental material reviewed by: Donald A. Grinde, Jr., Professor of Transnational/American Studies at the State University of New York at Buffalo.

Photo Credits: Cover EyeOn/Universal Images Group/Getty Images; pp. 4–5 Maksimilian/ Shutterstock.com; p. 7 DEA Picture Library/De Agostini Picture Library/Getty Images; pp. 9, 18 De Agostini Picture Library/De Agostini Picture Library/Getty Images; p. 11 Mortiz Steiger/Photographer's Choice/Getty Images; p. 12 Ptcamn~commonswiki/Wikimedia Commons; p. 13 Alex Covarrubias/Wikimedia Commons; p. 14 javarman/Shutterstock.com; p. 15 Kenneth Garrett/National Geographic Magazines/Getty Images; pp. 17, 21 (right) De Agostini Picture Library/ De Agostini/Getty Images; p. 19 David Hiser/National Geographic Magazines/Getty Images; p. 20 alessandro0770/Shutterstock.com; p. 21 (left) DEA/G. DAGLI ORTI/De Agostini/Getty Images; p. 22 Bridgeman Art Library/Getty Images; p. 25 Universal History Archive/Universal Images Group/Getty Images; p. 27 Tati Nova photo Mexico/Shutterstock.com; p. 28 Marilyn Angel Wynn/ Nativestock/Getty Images; p. 29 Rick Lew/The Image Bank/Getty Images.

Library of Congress Cataloging-in-Publication Data

Long, Erin, 1983- author.
 Aztec / Erin Long.
    pages cm. — (Spotlight on Native Americans)
 Includes index.
 ISBN 978-1-5081-4135-8 (pbk.)
 ISBN 978-1-5081-4136-5 (6 pack)
 ISBN 978-1-5081-4138-9 (library binding)
 1. Aztecs—Juvenile literature. I. Title.
 F1219.73.L65 2016
 972—dc23
                              2015028132

Manufactured in the United States of America

CPSIA Compliance Information: Batch #BW16PK: For Further Information contact Rosen Publishing, New York, New York at 1-800-237-9932

CONTENTS

THE HISTORY OF NATIVE PEOPLE

CHAPTER 1

The lands of North America have been home to Native American peoples for thousands of years. Ancestors of Native Americans occupied the land long before Europeans arrived. They lived throughout North America, from Canada to Central America. The Aztecs are a Native American people who arrived in the Valley of Mexico about 900 years ago.

Ancestors of the Aztec people—as well as all Native American peoples—probably came from eastern parts of Asia. Their **migrations** likely occurred during a cold period called an **ice age**. During this time, sea levels were much lower than they are today. In fact, sea levels were so low that the area between northeastern Asia and Alaska was dry, making a land bridge. People were able to walk between the continents using this land bridge.

Scientists aren't sure exactly when these migrations took place, but it was more than 12,000 years ago. In the thousands of years since then, water levels rose. The land bridge between Asia and the Americas was covered. Today, this area is called the Bering Strait.

This photo shows the coast of the Bering Sea, which was an area that was dry long ago. It sits between Alaska and Siberia, which is a part of northern Asia.

THE VALLEY OF MEXICO

CHAPTER 2

Around 10,000 years ago, Earth's climate warmed and became similar to conditions we have today. The first peoples in North America moved around the continent in small groups, hunting wild animals and collecting plants. These groups slowly spread out and lost contact with each other. Eventually, they developed separate **cultures** and adopted lifestyles that suited their **environment**.

The first cities in and around present-day Mexico appeared more than 3,000 years ago. In the Valley of Mexico, the city of Teotihuacán dominated central Mexico and its **city-states** from around 100 BC to AD 650. During that time, it was one of the largest cities in the world. The people of Teotihuacán became wealthy through the control of valuable trade goods and routes. They also benefited from their advanced systems of agriculture.

Teotihuacán eventually became less powerful. Náhuatl-speaking peoples, including the ancestors of the Aztecs, moved south from northwestern Mexico or possibly from the southwestern United States. By around 1200, they were established in the Valley of Mexico. They founded the city of Tenochtitlán in 1325. The city was on an island in Lake Texcoco. Just 100 years after founding Tenochtitlán, the Aztecs were the most powerful people in Mexico.

Tenochtitlán was built on an island. The water surrounding the city was a good defensive barrier.

THE SPANISH ARRIVE

CHAPTER 3

The Aztecs prospered for almost two centuries before Europeans first arrived in their part of the world. European ships reached North America around 1500. The first explorers were Spanish, who brought guns and horses. These tools were new to the Americas and gave the Spanish a great advantage over native peoples. They took over land in the present-day southeastern United States and Mexico and forced the Native Americans to work for them.

The Spanish reached Mexico in 1519. In 1521, they conquered the Aztec Empire and destroyed Tenochtitlán. They immediately began building Mexico City on the same site. Christian **missionaries** arrived soon after to convert and educate the now-conquered Aztecs. These missionaries helped create a written form of the Náhuatl language. This eventually became an official language of the Spanish Empire in the Americas.

Native Americans suffered greatly after coming into contact with Europeans. They contracted illnesses such as smallpox and measles. Having never been exposed to these diseases before, they had no chance of surviving them. At least half of all Native Americans died as a result. A smallpox epidemic from 1519 to 1520 killed millions in the Aztec Empire.

This artwork shows Hernán Cortés meeting the Aztec emperor Montezuma II, also known as Moctezuma II. Cortez was the **conquistador** who led the defeat of the Aztec Empire.

LIVING IN WHITE SOCIETY

CHAPTER 4

Native American groups, including the Aztecs, faced many difficulties after Europeans arrived and took over their lands. The Spanish tried to stamp out Aztec culture and force the Aztecs to join Spanish society. In 1696, the Spanish tried to prevent people from speaking Náhuatl. By the 1770s, writing the language was also discouraged. Only Spanish was taught in schools for most of the 20th century.

In North America, Native Americans were expected to adopt the ways and habits of white settlers. Native Americans on **reservations** endured poverty and very low standards of living. In the 1970s, the American Indian Movement (AIM) organized large protests that attracted attention worldwide. Many native groups formed their own governments, which allowed them to regain control over their lives and rights.

Aztec **descendants** in the 20th century were poorer and lived in more rural areas than other ethnic groups. In the 1990s, the Mexican government's policies toward native peoples improved. Today, Náhuatl is recognized as a national language in Mexico. Agencies have been created to promote and protect native communities. Today, many descendants of Aztec people live in Mexico's rural countryside. Aspects of traditional life, as well as the Náhuatl language, continue there today.

Though the Aztecs don't exist as a people today, their descendants and other Náhuatl-speaking groups are known today as the Nahuas. Their population numbers about 1.5 million.

THE HISTORY OF THE WORLD

CHAPTER 5

Ancient cultures told origin stories that explained the history of the world. Origin stories tell a tale of creation, explaining how the world and life on it began. The Aztecs believed that the earth was created and destroyed four times.

The fifth world was created by gods named Quetzalcoatl and Tezcatlipoca. They found the earth covered with water. Only a giant monster lived there. The gods tore the monster in two. The upper part of his body became land, and the lower part was thrown into the sky. It became the stars.

This artwork shows the Aztec gods that symbolize life and death.

Two other gods, Nanahuatzin and Tecuciztecatl, threw themselves into fire, becoming the sun and the moon. Quetzalcoatl then created humans. He went to the underworld of the dead and gathered old bones. He ground them up, sprinkled them with his own blood, and created the first people—the wandering Aztecs.

The wandering Aztecs called themselves Mexica. They began their journey at a place called Aztlan. Their god instructed them to leave Aztlan, and they traveled for many years. They knew they would recognize their new home by a sign—an eagle perched on a cactus with a snake in its beak.

This is the Mexican coat of arms, which displays part of the Aztec origin story.

RISING TO POWER

CHAPTER 6

The Aztecs arrived in the Valley of Mexico around 1168. The land was already occupied by descendants of the Toltecs. They were an advanced warrior society that ruled Mexico from the 10th to the 12th century. The Aztecs said they were descended from the Chichimecs, who were a wild, wandering, and warlike people.

Tenochtitlán ruins

The Aztecs eventually settled near the city of Culhuacan. The people there ruled the Aztecs, who were hired as soldiers to help defeat neighboring tribes in battle. A chief from the city of Culhuacan gave his daughter to an Aztec chief to marry. But she was **sacrificed** to the Aztec god Huitzilopochtli. War broke out between the people of Culhuacan and the Aztecs, and the Aztecs fled to the island in the middle of Lake Texcoco. Here, they saw an eagle perched on a cactus with a snake in its mouth! They had found their home. They began building in 1325 and named the city Tenochtitlán.

The Aztecs became very powerful once they built their own city. Aztec warriors began conquering neighboring tribes. During the mid-1400s, the Aztecs formed something called the Triple Alliance. Three city-states, Tenochtitlán, Texcoco, and Tlacopan, ruled over 12 million people in the Valley of Mexico.

People ruled by the Triple Alliance were required to pay **tribute** to their leaders. They had to send feathers, food, jewelry, slaves, and other valuables to Tenochtitlán twice a year.

AN ORGANIZED SOCIETY

CHAPTER 7

In the Aztec culture, each person knew their place in society from birth. Nobles owned land, ran the government, and were in charge of the army. They were at the top of society, and they were born into their class. Priests were also important because it was thought they were able to talk to the gods.

Merchants and artisans were next in society. This included stonemasons and feather workers. Next were common people, such as farmers, soldiers, and laborers. Finally, the lowest people in society were slaves. Slaves were people captured in war, but sometimes Aztecs sold themselves into slavery if they couldn't make a living. Commoners could become slaves if they didn't pay their taxes, but they could also rise in society to become a soldier or priest.

Aztec warriors were important in society. Many came from the noble classes. Some came from the lower classes, too. Warriors dressed according to their rank in the army. Eagle warriors, the top-ranking warriors, wore eagle feathers and helmets shaped like eagle heads.

Montezuma II, who is shown here, ruled the Aztec Empire from 1502 to 1520. As an emperor, he was the most powerful person in Aztec society.

FOOD, CLOTHING, SHELTER

CHAPTER 8

A person's place in society determined what kind of house they lived in and what kind of clothes they wore. Nobles lived in large stone homes with many rooms. Common people lived in huts made from clay bricks and straw roofs. Nobles were the only people who wore colorful clothing decorated with feathers, beads, and precious stones. Common people's clothing was simpler. Women wore skirts and a special kind of blouse, while men wore loincloths and capes.

The Aztec people were a farming society. However, they had to expand their land, as they had built their city on a small island.

Aztec home

They used floating gardens, or chinampas. They wove reeds together to form a raft-like structure, then put soil on top of it. The chinampas were anchored in shallow water and ready to be planted. Aztecs grew corn, beans, onions, peppers, tomatoes, squash, and many kinds of fruit. People used chinampas for their personal gardens and to grow flowers.

One favorite food was **tamales**, which people ate during their wedding. The Aztecs also ate fish, duck, and turkey. Only nobles were allowed to hunt bigger animals.

Remains of chinampas still exist in the southern part of Mexico City.

AZTEC ART AND WRITINGS
CHAPTER 9

Much art was created in Aztec society because they believed art was a way to communicate with and honor their gods. Aztec art was rooted in the Toltec culture. Sculptors carved calendars, gods and goddesses, and animal figurines from stone. They used precious stones to create beautiful **mosaics**. Aztec jewelry was made with gold and jewels. Even common household items, such as bowls, were beautiful examples of art. However, the artform valued above all else was feather work. Artisans

Aztecs carved elaborate calendars, such as the one pictured here.

used feathers from tropical birds, such as parrots, macaws, quetzals, and hummingbirds, to create elaborate headdresses and capes.

Aztec priests kept detailed records using picture books called codices. A codex was made by folding deerskin or paper made from bark into books. Painters made dyes from plants and ashes. Then, the writer of a codex, who was usually a priest, painted their stories into the book using a picture-based writing system. For example, a shield and arrows meant war. Footprints told of a journey. A cactus on a rock represented Tenochtitlán. Aztec codices were beautiful works of art and are a great source of information about Aztec society.

Aztec codices were destroyed after the Spanish took over. However, 15 codices still exist today. We can read them to learn more about Aztec culture.

GODS AND GODDESSES

CHAPTER 10

Religion in Aztec society was based on a system of gods and goddesses—and the Aztecs believed in many. Some historians believe they may have had over 1,600 gods! The number may have grown as Aztecs expanded their empire—they added gods from the cultures of people they conquered to their own belief system.

Aztecs believed their gods controlled all aspects of life. Some gods were more important than others. The chief god was Tonatiuh, the old sun god. Quetzalcoatl was the god of creation and the wind. Huitzilopochtli was the god of the sun, war, and sacrifice. Tlaloc was the god of rain, which was needed to grow crops. Two temples in the center of Tenochtitlán honored these important gods.

According to Aztec beliefs, each person had three souls. The way a person died determined how long it would take their souls to travel to the underworld. The souls of people who died ordinary deaths traveled for four years. People who were sacrificed or who had died in war went straight to the heavens. It only took 80 days for their souls to complete their journey. Bodies were buried with burial goods, such as tools and weapons, which were meant to help the souls as they traveled.

Quetzalcoatl, whose name means "feathered serpent," was an important Aztec god. He had special meaning for priests and was the god of creation, the wind, learning, books, and more.

SACRIFICES TO THE GODS
CHAPTER 11

Because the gods controlled all aspects of life, the Aztecs felt they needed to keep them happy. One way they did this was by making offerings to the gods through sacrifices. They sacrificed animals, such as jaguars, eagles, and dogs. They also sacrificed people. The Aztecs believed it was the people's task to sacrifice themselves to keep the sun moving and the world going. Their sun god, Huitzilopochtli, fought a daily battle in the sky. They felt human blood was a necessary food for the sun to continue rising.

During a human sacrifice, a person was selected for death, and then killed during a **ritual** ceremony. Sacrifices were only carried out as a religious ritual by priests in temples. The type of sacrifice depended upon which god was being honored. To honor Huitzilopochtli, the **victim** was placed on a sacrificial stone, which was usually at the top of a temple. A priest used a knife made from obsidian, a special stone, to cut open their abdomen. Then, the priest cut out the victim's heart and presented it to the sun while it was still beating. Other gods were honored through different kinds of sacrifices.

An Aztec warrior who caught an enemy used in a sacrifice (shown here) was greatly honored. His reward was to rise a step in Aztec society.

NAHUA PEOPLE TODAY

CHAPTER 12

Life completely changed for the Aztecs once the Spanish arrived in the early 16th century. Their government was destroyed, and their trade-based economy was replaced by the economy the Spanish established. Some native people, including the Aztecs, became Christians after the Spanish conquest.

Aztec culture has lived on through the Náhuatl language. Most people who speak this language live in the Mexican states of Guerrero and Hidalgo. The problems that Nahuas face today are the same as those experienced by many Native Americans. They're poor and live in rural areas without enough hospitals or schools. Many men, both young and old, move to the cities in hopes of finding work or joining the army.

Today, many modern-day Nahuas live in one-room houses with dirt floors. Each home has a garden, where the people farm the same food as their ancestors. In many places, modern homes are being built, so some villages finally have electricity and running water.

Nahua women weave clothing by hand, and many people still wear traditional clothing. Traditional clothing is also worn during ceremonies, which are often held around the time crops are planted and harvested.

Aztec culture is strongly felt in dances and celebrations. The Volador Dance asks the gods to end a **drought**. Attached by ropes, men dressed as birds swing around a pole until they are lowered to the ground. A man stands on top of the pole, dancing and playing instruments.

KEEPING CULTURE ALIVE

CHAPTER 13

The 1500s was the height of the Aztec civilization. Though that society no longer exists, the Aztec **heritage** and spirit can be easily seen in modern Mexican culture. Spanish, the main language of Mexico, uses many Aztec words, such as *tomate*, *chocolat*, and *tamale*.

Aztec rug

Many ruins of Aztec temples have been turned into museums, such as the Templo Mayor Museum in Mexico City. It contains objects found in the nearby Aztec temple. Many Aztec objects are held in the National Museum of Anthropology in Mexico City. Famous Mexican artists, such as Diego Rivera, have created artwork using Aztec symbols, faces, and scenes. Visitors to Mexico can buy traditional Aztec crafts, such as woven cloth, carved wood, and pottery. Since the 1960s, many Nahuas in Guerrero have been making paintings of rural scenes on amate bark paper, which is a traditional paper used by the Aztecs.

The Aztec people played an enormous role in the history of modern-day Mexico. Although an Aztec nation doesn't exist today, the contributions of the Aztec people live on in many aspects of modern Mexican culture.

Making traditional Aztec crafts and wearing traditional clothing are ways the Nahuas can celebrate their heritage.

GLOSSARY

city-state: A city that, with its surrounding territory, forms an independent state.

conquistador: A person who travels to a foreign place and takes over the land and its people, especially a Spanish conqueror of Mexico and Peru in the 16th century.

culture: The arts, beliefs, and customs that form a people's way of life.

descendant: Proceeding from people who lived long before you.

drought: A long period of time during which there is very little or no rain.

environment: The natural world.

heritage: Traditions and objects of value passed down through several generations.

ice age: A time marked by very cold temperatures over a long period of time.

migration: Movement of people to a new area.

missionary: A person who tries to teach others their religion.

mosaic: A picture or pattern produced by arranging small, colorful pieces of stone, tile, or glass.

reservation: Land set aside by the government for a specific Native American group or groups to live on.

ritual: A religious ceremony.

sacrifice: The act of taking a person or animal's life as an offering to a god.

tamale: A Mexican dish of meat wrapped in a cornmeal dough, which is steamed or baked in corn husks.

tribute: An act, statement, or gift that is meant to show respect.

victim: A living creature killed as a religious sacrifice.

FOR MORE INFORMATION

BOOKS

Apte, Sunita. *The Aztec Empire*. New York, NY: Scholastic, 2010.

Cooke, Tim. *At Home with the Aztecs*. London, UK: Brown Bear Books, 2015.

Tieck, Sarah. *Aztec*. Edina, MN: ABDO Publishing, 2015.

WEBSITES

Due to the changing nature of Internet links, PowerKids Press has developed an online list of websites related to the subject of this book. This site is updated regularly. Please use this link to access the list: www.powerkidslinks.com/sona/aztc

INDEX